1988 - 2014

105 Thornashire Court
Richmond
July 1988 - Sept 1993

7 Gamebird Court
Manakau-Sabot
Sept 1993 - June 2014

RICHMOND
IN COLOR

Profiles of America

RICHMOND
in Color

Text by
PARKE ROUSE, JR.

HASTINGS HOUSE · PUBLISHERS

New York, 10016

PUBLISHED 1978 BY HASTINGS HOUSE, PUBLISHERS, INC.

Library of Congress Cataloging in Publication Data

Rouse, Parke, 1915–
    Richmond in color.

 (Profiles of America)
  1. Richmond—Description. 2. Historic
buildings—Virginia—Richmond. 3. Richmond—
Buildings. 4. Richmond—History—Miscellanea.
I. Title.
F234.R54R68 975.5'451 78–26089
ISBN 0–8038–6358–6

Published simultaneously in Canada by
Saunders, of Toronto, Ltd., Don Mills, Ontario

Printed and bound in Hong Kong by Mandarin Publishers Limited

CONTENTS

Introduction   11

THE PLATES   31

Saint John's Church   33

Jacob Ege's Stone House   35

Wilton, Home of the Randolphs   37

The Capitol of Virginia   39

Houdon Statue of George Washington   41

Washington Statue in Capitol Square   43

The Governor's Mansion   45

Wickham House Garden   47

The Valentine Museum   49

Home of John Marshall   51

Interior of the Marshall House   53

Linden Row Houses   55

Old Hall of House of Delegates   57

Saint Paul's Church   59

The James River and Kanawha Canal Locks   61

White House of the Confederacy   63

Interior of Jefferson Davis's White House   65

The Fan District and Virginia Commonwealth University   67

Hollywood Cemetery   69

Robert E. Lee on Traveller   71

Jeb Stuart's Statue on Monument Avenue   73

Looking Across the James   75

Hotel Jefferson   77

Gardens of Agecroft Hall   79

Virginia House in Windsor Farms   81

Virginia Museum of Fine Arts   83
University of Richmond   85
World War I Carillon   87
Civic and Medical Centers   89
Richmond Coliseum   91
Skyline of Richmond   93
Commerce Surrounds the Capitol   95

6

I would like to express thanks to a number of people who have helped with information and photographs for this volume. They include Mr. Mike Stott of Design and Production Inc., formerly of the Richmond Chamber of Commerce; Ms. Polly Mason, manager of public relations of Richmond Metropolitan Chamber of Commerce; Ms. Meta Braymer of the University of Richmond; Mr. Frank McNally of the City of Richmond; Ms. Margaret Suydam of the National Society of the Colonial Dames of America; Mr. William T. Van Pelt of Virginia Commonwealth University; and Mr. Paul Murphy of Reynolds Metals Company. I am also indebted to Mrs. Ralph Catterall for her kindness in reading the text and to my wife, Betsy Gayle Rouse, for her assistance in countless unremembered ways. Of course, they are in no way responsible for any of the book's shortcomings.

PARKE ROUSE, JR.

RICHMOND
IN COLOR

RICHMOND
in Color

SOON AFTER the first permanent English settlers of America landed at
Jamestown in 1607, Christopher Newport and John Smith made a voyage
up the James River to the fall line. In May of 1607 they reached the present
site of Richmond, and the explorers with twenty followers came ashore and
explored the region of east Richmond which has since been known as Powhatan
Hill.

From that time on, "the falls of the James" were a well known site in
Virginia's geography. In 1634 the upland region around the fall line was
designated by the Virginia Assembly as Henrico shire, and a county seat was
established at Varina, a peninsula jutting into the James some fifteen miles
below the fall line.

Actually, Richmond began to grow significantly only in 1742, when
Henrico's county seat was moved from Varina to a riverside site laid out nine
years earlier for its owner, William Byrd II, at the fall line. A wooden Henrico
Parish church, now known as St. John's, was built in 1741 and expanded later,
giving the name Church Hill to the area. Nearby ran a creek, now obliterated
by storm sewers, known as Shockoe and creating the valley known as Shockoe
Bottom.

The squires of the area from the 1600s until after the Revolution were
the three William Byrds—father, son, and grandson. The first came about
1670 to take over his uncle Thomas Stegge's plantation below the falls, in the
present South Richmond. The second, the gifted "Black Swan of West over,"
chose to move his seat to Westover, nearer to the capital at Williamsburg.
But the third, born in 1728, built a handsome plantation, Belvidere, on the
James near the present Oregon Hill and in 1768 divided his lands and sold
them as building sites in a widely-promoted lottery.

It was William Byrd II in 1733 who first foresaw the growth of a sea-port
city at the falls of the James. He named it Richmond for the hillside city of

that name in Surrey County on the Thames near London.

Richmond's importance increased in the 1770s as relations between Virginia and King George III deteriorated. In March 1775, rebellious lawmakers from throughout the colony held a convention there to escape the prying eyes of His Majesty's Royal Governor in Williamsburg. Tiny Richmond was about to enter the mainstream of Revolutionary America.

At that convention in Henrico Parish Church, the Virginia colony was pushed towards revolution by Patrick Henry, the fiery red-haired delegate from Hanover. Daring his colleagues to take a firm stand against imperialism, he added: "Is life so dear or peace so sweet as to be purchased at the price of chains and slavery? Forbid it, almighty God! I know not what course others may take; but as for me, give me liberty or give me death!" From that moment, opinion in Virginia moved more rapidly toward revolution.

In the war that followed, Richmond and its commerce suffered acutely, but its importance had been established. James River traffic rose as settlement spread inland from Tidewater. Though once the western frontier of the colony, Richmond increasingly attracted commerce in the 1700s for its pivotal river site, midway between the inland Piedmont and the coastal Tidewater. As William Byrd II had written in 1733, Richmond, "being the uppermost landing of James River," was "naturally intended for marts, where the traffic of the outer inhabitants must centre." A city was being born.

Of all its civic deities, however, Richmond owes most to Thomas Jefferson, and not to Byrd. It was Jefferson who persuaded the Virginia Assembly in 1779 to move the seat of government from Williamsburg to the inconspicuous tobacco port near Shockoe's Creek. From that time onward Richmond's progress was rapid.

Not that Jefferson had any attachment for the town at the fall line of the James. He was instead an upcountry man, with a fondness for mountains. It was simply Richmond's location which won him. "Richmond, in the County of Henrico ... is more safe and central than any other Town situated on navigable water," read the bill which Jefferson drafted. After long debate, the Assembly agreed.

Today—200 years after Richmond's "anointment"—it is interesting to consider why this city got the nod over Petersburg, Newcastle on the Pamunkey, Fredericksburg, and other ports. Or why the legislators would leave Williamsburg for some raw new village 50 miles farther west in Virginia.

The answer lies in the fact that Virginia in 1779 faced British invasion. The capital at Williamsburg was exposed to attack by British warships in College Creek. In fact, a few days after the Assembly met in May 1779, a

British force actually entered the Capes and attacked Suffolk and Portsmouth. This convinced many lawmakers that a more "safe and central" site was needed.

But Jefferson was thinking in more positive terms. As early as 1761 he'd tried to persuade Assemblymen to move the capital westward. He tried again in the Assemblies of 1772 and 1776, using the argument that the seat of government should be nearer the growing western counties.

Richmond's choice was advanced when Jefferson was elected by the Assembly on June 1, 1779, to succeed Patrick Henry as second governor of the Commonwealth.

The House of Delegates on June 5 passed Jefferson's bill, and the measure reached a vote in the Senate a week later. Benjamin Harrison V, Speaker of the House of Delegates, reported the Delegates' action to the Senate and asked for its concurrence.

> . . . . . the equal Rights of the said Inhabitants require that such Seat of Government should be as nearly central to all as may be, having a Regard only to Navigation, the Benefits of which are necessary for promoting the Growth of a Town sufficient for the Accommodations of those who resort thereto, and able to aid the Operations of Government: And it has been also found inconvenient in the Course of the present War, where Seats of Government have been so situated as to be exposed to the Insults and Injuries of the publick Enemy, which Dangers may be avoided and equal Justice done to all the Citizens of this Commonwealth by removing the Seat of Government to the Town of Richmond, in the County of Henrico, which is more safe and central than any other Town situated on navigable Water . . . . "

For ten months after the Assembly chose Richmond, Jefferson and Virginia's government remained in Williamsburg. This allowed time to inform Virginia's county courts of the impending move. Time was also needed to find quarters for the Governor and Assembly in Richmond and to acquire "six whole Squares of Ground surrounded each of them by four Streets" in "an open and airy part" of Richmond for the postwar building of the Capitol, Governor's Mansion, and other prescribed buildings.

Jefferson and his Council of State chose April 7 to 23, 1780, as moving days. Soon oxen and horses in Williamsburg began drawing cartloads of boxes and barrels to College Landing on College Creek, close by the Capitol. John Williams sailed upriver with the first shipment about April 8, followed by Henry Burch in the schooner *Eastern Shore Betsey* on May 28, carrying the stores of the Board of Trade. Finally, Samuel Solomon took up the last shipment on a "flatt" or barge on June 12, towed by a sailing ship.

A few of the objects hauled to Richmond still survive after 200 years. Chief among them is the Speaker's chair of the House of Burgesses, which now sits in its former place in the reconstructed colonial Capitol in Williamsburg. Also taken from Williamsburg's Capitol to Richmond was the cast iron stove which Lord Botetourt used as royal governor of Virginia in 1768-70, now also back in Williamsburg. The State Library has a few of the lawbooks and reference books which belonged to the Council's library in Williamsburg, some bearing the Council's bookplate.

In Richmond, the Assembly found space in two wooden warehouses at Pearl (now Fourteenth) and Cary Street, close to the prospective site of Mayo's wooden bridge across the James. The warehouses had belonged to the Scottish merchants, Cunningham and Sons, whose loyalist clerks had returned to Glasgow at the Revolution's outbreak. From this crude Capitol Virginia was governed from 1780 until the new Capitol was completed in 1788.

The first year in Richmond proved so hectic that Governor Jefferson declined re-election in 1781 and narrowly missed legislative censure. For soon after the first Virginia Assembly met in its temporary quarters in the fall of 1780, British forces under Benedict Arnold came up the James and sent Jefferson and his government fleeing westward to Albemarle. Richmond suffered "the Insults and Injuries of the publick Enemy" that Jefferson had hoped to avoid.

Maps of Richmond in the Revolution show few buildings, for the town had less than a thousand people. Except for Henrico Parish Church and a few dwellings on Church Hill, the place was made up of farms and woods, with a few tobacco warehouses dotting the roads, and a few docks jutting from the shores of the James and of Shockoe Creek.

Looking back on the town, historian John Daly Burk about 1810 recalled its beginning in 1781:

> The fist of the Legislature bestowed upon it the *magnificent* name of "city," but it was yet a city in embryo. It scarcely afforded sufficient accommodations for the officers of Government, of which it had but recently been made the seat. The public buildings were temporary and modest. In short, every thing there, except the grand and sublime features of natural beauty impressed by the Creator himself on the picturesque site, was in a state of infancy. Art had given to the place no means of defense whatever. It could be protected only by a force collected from distant and various points. The fancy, in picturing to itself the Metropolis of Virginia, even at that epoch, is apt to exaggerate realities.

Who would ennoble these "grand and sublime features" with a Capitol worthy of the new age which Americans foresaw? There was only one man, and he was in Paris. Embittered by gubernatorial disasters, Jefferson had gone to France in 1784 as the American minister, succeeding Franklin. It was he who would provide Virginia with a vision worthy of its future.

Once the war ended, the Assembly in 1784 was ready to proceed with plans for the Capitol. Two of the directors of the Public Buildings, James Buchanan and William Hay, in that year engaged a draftsman, Roy Randolph, to design a building to face the river on the hillside site of "Gunn's yellow house." For economy's sake, the Legislature decreed that it was to combine the governor's office, legislative halls, and General Courtroom in one building —a decision contrary to Jefferson's 1779 capitol scheme to house each branch in its own building, which plan was influenced by Jefferson's belief in the checks and balances afforded by a three-branched government.

Alarmed at the departure from Jefferson's plans, his secretary, William Short, wrote him from Richmond in 1784 to alert him in Paris that the Assembly suddenly seemed about to settle for an old-fashioned colonial Capitol, like the one in Williamsburg:

.... The Directors have contracted with an Undertaker [contractor], and Roy Randolph is to draw the Plan. I wished them very much to send to some Part of Italy for a Design and Workmen. A good model I think would be a very great public Utility, and the example of important Workmen would unquestionably be followed and be attended with very good consequences. But I do not think the Directors believe it is possible to build a more magnificent House than the Williamsburg Capitol. It seems impossible to extend their Ideas of Architecture beyond it ....

Despite the Assembly's desire to rush the Capitol, the directors of the Public Buildings remembered Jefferson's interest in the plans and sent him a proposed interior arrangement of the projected building, with a request for design ideas. On behalf of the directors, Messrs. Buchanan and Hay urged him to suggest a facade so the contractor and the bricklayer—both already engaged —could begin work.

Jefferson accepted and wrote back to Richmond that he had engaged an architect, C. L. Clérisseau, to prepare drafts of the desired building design. Two months later he wrote again to say he had settled on an ideal precedent for the Capitol:

There is at Nimes in the South of France a building, called the Maison Quarrée, erected in the time of the Caesars, and which is allowed without contradiction

15

to be the most perfect and precious remain of antiquity in existence. Its superiority over anything at Rome, in Greece, at Balbec or Palmyra is allowed on all hands . . . .

Jefferson became totally absorbed. Unrestrainedly, he wrote that he had spent hours gazing at the Maison Quarrée, "like a lover gazing at his mistress."

The Assembly meanwhile was anxious to go ahead with the long-delayed project, for peace had come. Accordingly, the directors of the Public Buildings approved the laying of the cornerstone on August 18, 1785, in the presence of Governor Patrick Henry and a large crowd. And to keep the project moving, they allowed the brickmasons to lay foundations at the agreed site, though they had received only a preliminary building plan from Jefferson at the time.

The foundations were laid for a building 118 feet wide and 148 feet deep. This was of the same proportion as the adaptation Jefferson sent of the Maison Quarrée, but it was larger. One early ill-effect was the inadequacy of the early columns, whose size was not at first correctly scaled to the enlarged building. On completion in 1789, the Capitol was by no means a total triumph, but at least it was a beginning. Returning from France in 1789, Jefferson hurried to Richmond to see his brainchild and then wrote to his ex-secretary, William Short, in Paris:

> Our new Capitol, when the corrections are made of which it is susceptible, will be an edifice of first-rate dignity. Whenever it shall be finished with the proper ornament belonging to it (which will not be in this age) it will be worthy of being exhibited along side the most celebrated remains of antiquity. Its extreme convenience has acquired it unusual approbation . . . .

In the chaos of post-Revolutionary Virginia, it was amazing that the Assembly could find money to build so large and handsome a temple—the first of many neo-classical public buildings to be built in America—but Jefferson had realized the need for some physical embodiment of the new age and had pushed the project through, against doubtful legislators. "How is a taste for a chaste and good style of building to be formed in our countrymen unless we seize all occasions which the erection of public buildings offer . . . ?" he wrote Edmund Randolph in 1785.

Like such port towns as Yorktown and Smithfield, Richmond stood on two levels: a low waterfront of docks, warehouses, and shipways, and a high-level residential area, on Church and Shockoe Hills. The chief glory of the site was these riverside heights, which recalled to literary minds the legendary seven hills of Rome.

The village's hub until 1788 was Henrico Parish Church, where Patrick Henry had made his "Liberty or Death" speech in 1775. Around it clustered houses built on lots first laid out in 1737 and extended as population grew. Then, on steep streets descending from Henrico Church to Shockoe Creek and the James, there were other Church Hill houses of tobacco merchants and warehousemen. In the river bottom, along wagon trails which converged at Pearl and Cary Street, stood such warehouses as Cunningham's, where the Capitol was temporarily housed from 1780 to 1789.

John Mayo operated a ferry across the James from Pearl (later Fourteenth) Street to Manchester, but as traffic increased, his son, John, Junior, replaced it in 1788 with a wooden bridge. Many bridges have succeeded the original structure at that site, but Mayo's wooden toll bridge was a landmark for many years.

To this embryo town from the Revolution until years afterward, farmers came to market from the fertile "black belt" south of the James, rolling or carting hogsheads of tobacco to be shipped abroad or to be made into pipe tobacco, snuff, cigars, or later into cigarettes. Other drays bearing cattle, wheat, skins, and lumber rolled in from the eastern counties over Country Road, which was renamed Main Street. Flatboats brought other produce down the James to Westham, several miles west of the town, above the fall line.

The road from Mayo's bridge led uphill from Shockoe Bottom to Broad Road, which went westward into Henrico and Hanover Counties.

A visitor to Richmond in 1783 was shocked by the rough dress and undecorous behavior of the General Assembly in its temporary wooden capitol. "This estimable assembly," wrote the Bavarian surgeon Johann Schoepf, met each day not quite "five minutes together. Some are leaving, others coming in, most of them talking of insignificant or irrelevant matters ... horse races, runaway Negroes, yesterday's play." The legislators "wore the same clothes in which one goes hunting or tends his tobacco fields," snorted Schoepf.

The Capitol was still incomplete when the Virginia Convention met in Richmond to ratify the Federal Constitution in June 1788; that body had to meet instead in Beaurepaire's Academy on Broad Street. However, the Capitol was finally ready for the General Assembly to meet there in October of 1788, though the roof leaked.

The Assembly's first sessions in Richmond had been hard ones, and others lay ahead. In those first crowded years it had granted incorporation to Liberty Hall Academy and to Hampden-Sydney and Transylvania Colleges; had ceded Virginia's Northwest Territory to the federal government; had given up territory to establish the Commonwealth of Kentucky; and had enacted

Jefferson's Statute of Religious Freedom. A monument at the intersection of Fourteenth and Cary Street—now a rundown area—marks the site where so much history was changed.

The town revived a little after victory at Yorktown in 1881 assured American independence. In that age of ship transport, the James River was a chief highway of Virginia. From the spreading central and western counties, quantities of tobacco and wheat were shipped downriver to market at Richmond. Some was distributed by carts in Virginia, but most was sent by sailing ships from Rocketts, the wharf area of lower Richmond, to coastal cities or to Europe. Richmond became a major port, in competition with Norfolk, Petersburg, and Alexandria.

To bypass the falls in the James, a canal was built from Bosher's Dam, seven miles above Richmond, to lower Main Street, in 1795. A few years later, the James River Canal was completed to Lynchburg so that flat-bottomed canal boats could go back and forth, pulled by mules. Under the leadership of John Marshall, Richmond's first citizen till he died in 1835, plans were pushed to link the upper James in Botetourt County with the Kanawha River in western Virginia, creating a trans-Allegheny canal system. However, the ambitious scheme was never realized. After the Civil War, railroads became dominant.

Leading Revolutionary figures frequented Richmond in those years. The convention to ratify the Constitution, meeting in 1788 in an auditorium on the site now occupied by the Medical College of Virginia, saw such giants as Madison, Monroe, Marshall, Patrick Henry, and Lighthorse Harry Lee. Among Richmond's lawyers were George Wythe and Edmund Randolph, while its leading editor in the Jeffersonian age was Thomas Ritchie, whose *Enquirer* was long a powerful Jeffersonian voice.

A celebrated confrontation between President Jefferson and Chief Justice John Marshall took place in Richmond in 1807 when Aaron Burr was tried for treason in the new Virginia Capitol. Marshall, who presided, issued a subpoena for the President's appearance in court, but Jefferson ignored it. The town was then divided between Jeffersonians and Federalists, the latter led by Marshall. In Marshall's reign as Richmond's first citizen, the town had a Whig flavor, though it later became a stronghold of conservative Democrats.

The Richmond of these years was a sleepy Southern town extending for a dozen city blocks along Main and Broad Streets from Church Hill to Capitol Hill. Once the Capitol was built, population shifted westward to the fashionable "Court End" of town. The John Marshalls built at Ninth and Marshall Streets, while the Edmund Randolphs lived at Tenth and Capitol Streets, and

George Wythe, chancellor of the Virginia Court of Chancery, at Fifth and Franklin Streets. An apt law student of Wythe's was Henry Clay, who went west to Kentucky in 1798.

The town was grief-stricken in 1811 when its new theatre burned with the loss of 61 persons, including Governor George William Smith. A church designed by Robert Mills was built on the site as a memorial to the victims and is now the chapel of the Medical College of Virginia.

Always theatre-loving, Richmond had a succession of other play-houses, where such stars as Edwin Booth, Joe Jefferson, Minnie Maddern Fiske, Sarah Bernhardt, and Otis Skinner performed.

Great political power centered in Richmond during the years of the Richmond Junto, a coterie of Democrats headed by Chief Justice Spencer Roane of the Virginia Supreme Court of Appeals until his death in 1822. Other members were Dr. John Brockenbrough, president of the Bank of Virginia, Congressman Andrew Stevenson, who became Speaker of the U. S. House of Representatives from 1827 to 1834; and Editor Ritchie of the *Enquirer*. The influence of Richmond and Virginia spread far.

A leading Richmond tobacco merchant of early 19th century Richmond was John Allan, who lived at Fifth and Main. In 1811 he and his wife took into their home three-year-old Edgar Allan Poe, on his mother's death and reared him. Poe went to school in Richmond and abroad, but he regarded Richmond as home during the rest of his chaotic life. The struggling writer returned to Richmond in 1835 to help edit the *Southern Literary Messenger*. A year later he married 13-year-old Virginia Clemm, before moving north, where he achieved considerable fame. After Virginia's death he returned to Richmond in 1849 and proposed to his childhood sweetheart, Elmira Royster, who had been widowed. However, he died in Baltimore on his way to Richmond for the wedding.

The Richmond of Poe's lifetime remained a river town. At Fifth Street on the river was the State Armory, and nearby grew up several foundries which fed local industries. These produced cannon, locomotives, marine engines, sugar mills, and metal for railway ties and building. Nearly a dozen such foundries had developed by the 1850s, including the Tredegar Iron Works on the James near Fifth Street, which was to supply much of the metal for the Confederacy in the Civil War.

Richmond's large nineteenth century flour mills utilized the water-power of the James to turn their wheels. Such mills as the Gallego, the Columbian, Bragg's, and the Dunlop ground wheat brought downriver by canal boats from Lynchburg and the Piedmont. In turn, the mills shipped their products down the James to coastal ports. Other users of water-power were paper mills, distilleries, and cotton and woollen mills. In Shockoe slip and along the James worked dozens of carriage-makers, soap and candle-makers, farm-machine manufacturers, and tobacconists.

Many artisans worked in Manchester, a town originally called Rocky Ford, which lay across the James, at the other end of Mayo's Bridge. It became a part of Richmond in 1910.

Around Capitol Square grew churches, hotels, banks, and offices of the town, which, though styled by the General Assembly in 1782 as "the city of Richmond," was not incorporated as a city until 1842. Churches vied to see which could build the tallest steeple, visible for miles to those who approached by river or road. A handsome city hall was built in 1818 to a design by Robert Mills, later torn down, and a theatre was designed by the famous Benjamin Latrobe, though never built.

It was an age of statuary, and Richmond was beautified by monuments. The first was Houdon's magnificent standing figure of Washington, commissioned by the General Assembly in 1795 and placed in the rotunda of the Capitol. The second was Crawford's equestrian statue of Washington, whose cornerstone was laid in 1852 in the presence of President Zachary Taylor. Many others came as Richmond's scale and amenities grew.

Literature and learning spread in the long peace between the War of 1812 and the Civil War of 1861.

Charles Dickens came in 1842, to stay at the Exchange Hotel and to write later of his dismay at slavery and his delight in "the mounds of ices and the bowls of mint-julep and sherry cobbler they make in these latitudes." Eleven years later, William Thackeray came to give a lecture on early English writers at the Athenaeum on Marshall Street. Later Thackeray in 1857 wrote a novel of 18th century Virginia, *The Virginians*.

Besides its Athenaeum, Richmond had other literary institutions. In addition to several private schools, often called seminaries or academies, it had by the 1850s two free schools: the Lancasterian School, supported by the city, and the Armory School, supported by generous citizens.

There was also Richmond College, incorporated in the city in 1842 as successor to the former Virginia Baptist Seminary. A Freedmen's Bureau school for blacks, begun after the Civil War, grew into Virginia Union University. Finally, there was the medical college of Hampden-Sydney, which moved from Prince Edward County and in 1845 built an Egyptian-style building. It was to merge in 1913 with University Medical College as the State-supported Medical College of Virginia, today a unit of Virginia Commonwealth University.

By 1858 Richmond had also a public library of 2,000 volumes, conducted by "a company of gentlemen," and a gas-lighted theatre at the corner of Broad and Seventh Streets where plays and musicales were performed. Traveling troupes from New York and London frequently came to town for brief seasons of repertory.

In spite of all this, Richmond lagged behind Baltimore in growth, and this worried boosters. Baltimore businessmen in the 1840s had organized the Baltimore and Ohio Railway, whose main line went westward through northern Virginia and Maryland to Wheeling, on the banks of the Ohio River. Built to compete with New York's Erie Canal system for western trade, the B & O quickly took much Ohio Valley commerce from the James River and Kanawha Canal system.

By the 1840s, Richmond clearly lacked long-haul railroads to compete with Baltimore's and New York's. It had short lines to Norfolk, Danville, Staunton, Washington, and southwest Virginia, but it needed longer regional facilities. Editor J. W. Randolph was somewhat defensive in his summary of the city's progress in the *Richmond Business Directory* for 1858-59.

"There is nothing wanting to make Richmond a great and flourishing city," he wrote, "abounding in wealth and manufactures of all kinds, but a little more of public-spiritedness and energetic perseverance on the part of the citizens. Let them foster and encourage every enterprise calculated to advance the interests of the city, and Richmond must eventually become one of the largest, wealthiest, most intelligent and influential cities of the Union."

In the census of 1860, Richmond ranked thirteenth in the nation in the value of its manufacturing. Its 300 plants hired 7,316 people and produced $12,000,000 in goods yearly. Much of this was to be lost in the burning of Richmond in the war to come.

In retrospect, it is clear that Richmond in 1858 was a thriving community. Only two defects clouded its ambitions. One was slavery and the other was its dependence on canals instead of the fast new railroads. Both defects were to be overcome, though at tragic cost, by the war which broke out in 1861.

When the Virginia Convention gathered at the Capitol in February 1861 to consider secession, the town had grown to 37,968 people. At first Virginia was cautious about leaving the Union. "Surely," Governor John Letcher told the body, "no people have been blessed as we have been, and it is melancholy to think that all is now about to be sacrificed on the altar of passion." But after President Lincoln in April called on the states to provide troops to help put down the insurgents in South Carolina, the cry for secession grew.

After the Convention at the Capitol voted on April 17 to secede, flames of war soon enveloped Virginia. On April 23, Robert E. Lee stood in the House of Delegates chamber and took the oath as commander of Virginia's forces. "Trusting in almighty God, an approving conscience, and the aid of my fellow citizens," he told the Convention, "I devote myself to the service of my native State, in whose behalf alone will I ever again draw my sword."

By seceding, Virginia doomed herself to be the battleground of war, as events soon proved. The Confederacy in May 1861 moved its capital to Richmond, and President Jefferson Davis and his family occupied Dr. John Brockenbrough's mansion at Twelfth and Clay Streets. The Confederate congress met in the Capitol, and Confederate departments took over Main Street offices. John Stewart, a Scottish merchant, lent his house on Franklin Street to General Lee and his family. Richmond became, in the eyes of the world, "the capital of the Rebel government."

Overnight, the city became a noisy hive. Refugees thronged in from the Peninsula to escape the advance in 1861-62 of General George B. McClellan's Peninsula campaign, and faro parlors and saloons abounded. Gamblers, speculators, and prostitutes flourished. From her mansion on Church Hill, Unionist spy Elizabeth Van Lew encouraged the "underground railroad" and sent messages to Washington. After the Battle of Bull Run in July 1861, injured Confederates overflowed the city's makeshift hospitals. Within a year, 22 such factories and warehouses became medical facilities. A warehouse at the east end of town became the famous Libby military prison, later moved and exhibited at the Chicago World's Fair of 1876.

When the 80,000 Union troops of George McClellan in 1862 approached the alarmed town, Lee took command of the defenders and stood McClellan off in the bloody Seven Days' Battles. Cannonading could be heard constantly in the city, and streams of injured and dying men were brought into hospitals. Tiny Oakwood Cemetery alone received 18,000 dead.

Richmond's spirit remained high until 1864, when General Grant's harsh offensive against Richmond and Petersburg took effect. Even so, citizens sought to keep up a brave front with theatricals, parties, and church services. Confederate money became virtually worthless. By August 1864 flour was $400 a barrel, butter $8 a pound, and meat was unobtainable at any price.

The war made many heroes: Captain Sally Tompkins, who organized services to tend the ill in Richmond hospitals; General J.E.B. Stuart, who was wounded outside Richmond in 1864 and died in a house at 206 West Grace Street; Hetty Cary, who married Brigadier General John Pegram at St. Paul's in 1865 and was widowed three weeks later. But the supreme heroes after 1862 were Stonewall Jackson, who met his death at Chancellorsville in 1863, and Lee, who survived the war to become a legend.

The end came suddenly. While Jefferson Davis attended Sunday service at St. Paul's on April 2, 1865, a message came from Lee in Peterburg that he no longer could hold out against Grant's siege. Richmond must fall.

To keep warehouses of cotton and tobacco out of Federal hands, Confederate forces burned lower Main Street along the river. Soon flames spread out of control and engulfed nearby houses and shops. Looting broke out. Hungry people rushed ahead of the flames to grab food and goods out of doomed buildings. By morning, Confederate troops had completed the self-destruction and fled with the Confederate government south of the James River, burning their bridges behind them as the Federal army approached from the north.

Nine hundred houses had been burned, valued then at $4,000,000. Also destroyed were $30,000,000 of offices, factories, and other commercial buildings. "Never was there a sadder day in Richmond's history," wrote W. Asbury Christian, in his *Richmond: Her Past and Present*, "and may there never be another like it. Many of the citizens who before had plenty were now reduced to poverty. To us today it seems a thousand times better for the Federal troops to have used all the tobacco in Richmond than to have brought this awful calamity upon an already afflicted city." Eight days after the senseless waste, Lee surrendered to Grant at Appomattox.

As the Confederates left Richmond, Mayor Joseph Mayo sent a message to the Federal General Godfrey Weitzel outside Richmond. He asked that Federal troops take possession of the city "to preserve order and protect women and children and property." Weitzel's army marched in and gradually subdued the flames. Pillaging was brought under control, and the United States flag was raised over the Capitol again. Lincoln came to Richmond and was greeted by throngs of blacks.

From Richmond, the military governor, General John Schofield, soon began the slow process of Reconstruction decreed by Congress. Virginia became Military District 1, its ex-Confederates disenfranchised and suspect. The harsh years 1865 to 1870—bitter years of Reconstruction and of Richmond's occupation by Federal troops—were black ones for "the Mother of States and of Statesmen."

Blacks suffered most in the Reconstruction years. Freed by Lincoln's Emancipation Proclamation in 1863, many came from rural Virginia into Richmond in search of housing and jobs. Despite the schooling and legal advice given them by the Freedmen's Bureau, they became a heavy responsibility of the city and its people. A third of the population after the war was black.

Thanks to Richmond's ingrained sense of order and respect for law, the city survived the era of "Black Republican" rule with little bitterness. The lot of most Negroes remained meagre, however, until it was slowly raised by public education, jobs, and Federal policies in the century after Appomattox.

Richmond's artists and writers have left engaging pictures of the blacks in the years when sidewalk markets lined unpaved city streets in the indolent decades before World War I. The talented William Ludwell Sheppard in post-Appomattox years sketched bandannaed "mammies" selling possums and muskrats at stands, while their children hawked Christmas wreaths nearby. Many such line drawings enlivened the pages of *Harper's Weekly*, *Leslie's Illustrated Newspaper*, *Scribner's*, and *The Century* in the years before photoengraving. Welcome survivors of these vendors today are the flower sellers on the Boulevard.

Other Richmond citizens and scenes were depicted on canvas by Conrad Wise Chapman, Laurence and Thomas Sully, William James Hubard, John A. Elder, James Warrell, Edward Peticolas, James Ford, and George Cooke. Photographers' studios blossomed, like George S. Cook's on Main Street, and a host of partisan and denominational periodicals—a few in German—eked out an existence. In those days, many Americans knew Richmond only as the publication place of the *Southern Planter* and the *Southern Churchman*, both now dead.

Writers somehow bloomed in the miasma of Reconstruction. George W. Bagby, Thomas Nelson Page, Kate Langley Bosher, and Emma Speed Sampson wrote of the ties which knit together white masters and black servants. Mary Johnston looked backward for romance, while others tried to cope with the present. Intellectually and artistically, Richmond took the lead in setting the tone for a New South.

Richmond's revival came with the belching onrush of the railroad locomotive. The city was well situated as a rail center, and the boom which came in the 1880s lifted the city back to its prewar prosperity. Thanks to its foundries, the city was a natural site for locomotive-building. Provisional Governor Francis Pierpont in 1865 invited Northern capital to restore the lines destroyed in the war. By the 1880s rail-building was booming in Richmond.

The six short-line roads which served Richmond in 1880 had only 1,893 miles of track, but they rapidly grew. Through merger or extension they reached 3,368 miles in 1890. By that time or soon afterward, Richmond was served by the C & O, Norfolk and Western, Atlantic Coast Line, Seaboard,

Southern, and the Richmond, Fredericksburg, and Potomac. Until the advent of automobiles in the 1920s, Richmond prospered as a railway center.

Another rising industry was tobacco. The popularity of the cigarette in the 1870s led to the birth of forty Richmond cigarette factories. Together with the chewing- and smoking-tobacco plants, they were Richmond's top industry.

The postwar era spawned many small first generation tobacco industries, many of which were to merge or to fail as big business grew and competition grew in the twentieth century. Four firms reigned as the giants of Victorian Richmond: Allen and Ginter, James Thomas Jr., Patterson and Williams, and finally Thomas C. Williams, Jr., who had earlier been in business with Thomas and Patterson. In turn, they merged and disappeared as R. J. Reynolds, Phillip Morris, American Tobacco, Liggett and Myers, and Brown and Williamson appeared. Slowly, tobacco cultivation and sales moved southward to Durham, Winston-Salem, and Louisville, though Richmond kept a portion.

New wealth stimulated a lively social life in the gay nineties and the Edwardian years. With growth, the city developed a more stratified society, somewhat more urbane than most of the South except Charleston, New Orleans, Savannah, and a few other old cities. Industry spread, real estate boomed, and institutions like the Westmoreland and Commonwealth Clubs, the Richmond German, the Deep Run Hunt, the Virginia Historical Society, the Mozart Society, and the Valentine Museum came into their own.

The turn-of-century years produced a number of rich men, for the income tax had not been introduced, and business profits were often high. Millionaires like Thomas Branch, Joseph Bryan, Frederic Scott, and A. D. Williams set a pattern that was emulated in townhouses along Franklin and Grace Streets. Richmond's style was English and formal. Wages were low, and servants were plentiful, both upstairs and downstairs.

Many Jewish, Scottish, and Germanic descendants prospered, especially in baking, dry goods, and real estate. Several early Jewish families intermarried with gentiles and were absorbed in Richmond's dominantly Anglican society. Distinguished Richmonders today descend from these Jewish-Christian unions.

Nearly all well-brought-up Richmond children for many years went to private schools. Miss Phronie Pegram's school on Linden Row took both boys and girls, while Miss Virginia Randolph Ellett's—"Miss Jenny's"—was a school for young ladies on Linden Row. Richmond Female Institute became Westhampton College. Others were Mrs. Camm's school for boys and Dr. Wistar Archer's University School for young men, followed later by the prep schools of Captain Gordon McCabe, CSA, John Peyton McGuire, and Churchill Gibson Chamberlayne.

Miss Ellett and Dr. Chamberlayne were permanently influential, for their institutions came under Episcopal governance as St. Catherine's and St. Christopher's schools.

Richmond's private schools long contributed strongly to the city's homogeneity, more than any other influence, though their influence is now abated by population growth. Close ties between kinsmen and classmates have produced an inner circle of families, linked by marriage, church, and habits of speech and dress. These ties were reinforced when many of Richmond's young people went on to the University of Virginia, Hollins, and Sweet Briar. Today's Richmond is more pluralistic.

Fortunate Richmonders of the early 1900s enjoyed an active social life, spiced with visits to the Virginia springs and by rail trips to northern cities and southern resorts. Society had its fancy dress balls, its germans, its Deep Run Hunt races, its Virginia Boat Club races, and its Mozart Society concerts at the Mozart Academy and later at the Academy of Music and the City Auditorium.

So formalized did Richmond society become that names of its members were printed in 1893 in one of America's first social registers, the *Richmond Elite Directory*, reissued periodically through 1915. No other town of such small size in America had a social register.

The *Elite Directory* listed about 1,500 of Richmond's 80,000 people. These were its Society. Dancing was popular, and members of the Tuesday German, the Friday German, and the Arlington German were listed with those of the Richmond German. Also fashionable were Kermess balls in fancy dress, held at the Masonic Temple or Jefferson Hotel for the benefit of charity. Among Richmond belles were Nancy and Irene Langhorne, who became Lady Astor and Mrs. Charles Dana Gibson, and Judith Carrington, who became Mrs. Edward R. Stettinius.

Richmond enjoyed a railroad boom after the Civil War. Its pre-war population of 38,000 had grown to 64,000 by 1880, and by 1906 it had grown to 105,000—thanks to its steady movement westerly up the James. In 1910, the annexation of Manchester raised the total to 147,628 and necessitated extensions of the city's street railway system, begun in 1888 as one of the first electric lines in the nation. Another pioneer service was the telephone exchange, begun over a shoe factory on Main Street in 1879. It was the third in the United States.

In those days, before the advent of automobiles, residential areas followed trolley routes. After years' confinement to the present downtown and Fan district, settlement leaped westward. Trolley lines were laid across the Ninth

Street Bridge south to Manchester, across Marshall Street Viaduct east to Churchill Hill, through the Fan district and west to Forest Hill Park, Lakeside Zoo, and Westhampton; and north to Barton Heights and Ginter Park.

Although automobiles were not common until World War I, early city planners wisely provided a few wide thoroughfares like Broad Street, the Boulevard, and Monument Avenue. The creation of such parks as Monroe, Byrd, Chimborazo, and Bryan beautified the city, and the placement of trees and of statues honoring Lee, Jackson, Stuart, Jefferson Davis, Maury, Confederate soldiers and sailors, and A. P. Hill embellished it. The creation of two handsome rail depots—the Italianate Main Street and the neo-classical Broad Street (the latter the work of John Russell Pope) added distinction.

In the fan district beyond Monroe Park, Edwardian townhouses of brick, wood, and stone gave variety to the city. The Jefferson Hotel, built in 1895, and many Gothic and classical style churches further stimulated community pride.

Richmond from the 1780s onward became the hub of Virginia's intellectual, literary, and scientific life. Its newspapers have been especially influential from the day of Thomas Ritchie till the present. John Hampden Pleasants was a major figure as editor of the *Richmond Whig*, long a rival of Ritchie's *Enquirer*, and there have been other newspapers. Scholars, printers, and publishers have made Richmond a regional literary center. The city has one of the chief printing industries of the nation.

An interest in belles lettres became evident in the 1920s. In 1921 a group of literati launched *The Reviewer*, which for a year or so printed work by leading American and British writers of the time. Simultaneously, Richmond acquired talents of its own. Ellen Glasgow and James Branch Cabell were leading American novelists, while Douglas Freeman was an acclaimed biographer and editor. Others have continued in this tradition.

In the realm of music, John Powell was widely known as a pianist and composer, while John Treville LaTouche was a talented theatrical lyricist and author of *The Ballad of Baby Doe* and other stage works. Bill "Bojangles" Robinson was a celebrated tap dancer and film star.

Higher education has increasingly sought nourishment from Richmond's professional talent. Richmond College has grown into the University of Richmond, with a law school and graduate instruction. Social work training begun in 1917 by the College of William and Mary grew in 1968 into Virginia Commonwealth University, with the Medical College constituting its Life Sciences Division.

Union Theological Seminary, moved from Hampden-Sydney in 1898 to a site given by Major Lewis Ginter; Virginia Union University, begun after the Civil War as a Freedmen's Bureau school for blacks; and J. Sergeant Reynolds Community College, started in 1973, give Richmond a huge population of adult students.

Other facilities have expanded. The Virginia Museum was created in 1931 as the first State-supported in the nation, supplementing the facilities of the Valentine Museum, begun in 1892 by Mann Valentine II with a fine arts and archeological collection centered on Virginia. The Richmond Symphony was born in 1932, and the Richmond Ballet in 1957. To the performance facilities of the Mosque and the Richmond Stadium, the city in 1971 added the 12,000-seat Coliseum for conventions, concerts, and athletic events.

Major art exhibits, concerts, books, magazines, and academic achievements continue to call attention to Richmond as a creative community.

Ellen Glasgow before she died in Richmond in 1945 had foreseen "the retreat of agrarian culture before the conquests of the industrial revolution, and the slow and steady rise of the lower middle class." These movements, clearly evident after World War II, shook the staid city to its depths. Racial conflict flared as the old paternalistic order died, amid murmurs of social unrest. Richmond, in common with all of Virginia, lost something precious in the decline of manners, the weakening of home and religious influence, the quickening of life's pace.

Yet Richmond gained, too. In the long prosperity from World War II to the 1970s, its citizens lived better than they ever had. The city broadened its social base. Gradually its private schools, clubs, churches, and colleges opened their doors a little wider.

Like much of America, Richmond today is seeing the domination of civic and political affairs pass from a male white Protestant leadership to a widened white and black electorate. It is no longer a parochial Southern capital, but a spreading industrial giant, with all the advantages and problems industry brings.

As in all social evolution, Richmond's gains have been at the cost of losses. Beloved landmarks have gone or are threatened. Yet Richmond has tried to preserve its Tidewater Virginia character in a chaotic time, and it has partly succeeded. Deep-seated amity between races and ethnic groups has survived. To many, it is still a place of enviable charm, warmth and hospitality.

So gracious an old lady should be permitted her eccentricities, should she not? And besides, it would be futile to try to change her. As they say at St. John's Church, "Whom God hath joined together, let no man put asunder." It would be impossible to put asunder the blend of Jeffersonian simplicity and

28

Hamiltonian elitism in Richmond today. Despite the reminders of its romantic Confederate past, it is today a growing modern metropolis with all the headaches which success brings.

THE PLATES

SAINT JOHN'S CHURCH

The settlement which became Richmond began to grow in the 17th century along the banks of the James River at Shockoe Creek, at the river's falls. A few piers and warehouses appeared first. An English emigrant named Thomas Stegge in mid-century built his plantation house on the south shore of the river near that point, leaving his estate on his death to William Byrd I, who came to this frontier area of Henrico County about 1670.

Byrd's son, William Byrd II, who became a great planter and a scholar, in 1733 planned the city he called "Richmond," and three years later he laid it out. It covered massive Richmond Hill, which later became known as Church Hill after a frame Henrico Parish Church, built in 1741 on two lots given by Byrd for that purpose. Simultaneously, the courthouse of Henrico was moved to Richmond from its former site at Varina, about fifteen miles downriver on the James.

The church was enlarged in 1772 and later, and in the nineteenth century it was adorned with a belltower and the name St. John's, the latter to distinguish it from other churches in Richmond. Its moment of fame came in 1775, when a convention of Virginia delegates met there to consider complaints against the crown. There Patrick Henry made his famous "liberty or death" speech which presaged Virginia's call for revolution the next year.

Church Hill remained the center of Richmond until after 1780, when the Virginia Assembly chose nearby Capitol Hill to be the site of Virginia's seat of government. Thereafter, its importance slowly declined. Handsome new residences were built west of the Capitol, but Church Hill retained imposing residences of 18th and 19th century origin. Today the area is being restored by individual owners and by the Historic Richmond Foundation. St. John's remains an active parish of the Episcopal Church.

JACOB EGE'S STONE HOUSE, NOW THE POE MUSEUM

Typical of the simple houses of early Richmond is the stone cottage built about 1739 on Main Street by Jacob Ege, an emigrant from Wurttemberg, who had come to Richmond a year earlier. Built of rock dredged to deepen the James, it has the usual proportions of its era, with a second floor for bedrooms, ventilated by dormer windows facing onto the river not far away.

Ege, a cooper or tailor by trade, was typical of the many German and Alsatian artisans who came to early Richmond and throve there. He married Maria Dorothea Scherer, daughter of General Nicholas Scherer, who had come to Richmond from Hesse-Cassel about the same time as the Eges. Many French families, a few of them Huguenot refugees fleeing Catholic oppression in France's Protestant cities, also came to early Richmond.

Samuel Ege, son of Jacob and Dorothea, was a Henrico County representative to the Virginia convention to ratify the Constitution, held in Richmond in 1788. In his house he boarded James Monroe and other out-of-town lawmakers who came to Richmond annually after the city became Virginia's capital.

To preserve this unusual house, the Poe Foundation in the twentieth century acquired it as the Edgar Allan Poe Museum. Though the house has no known connection with Poe, it was a part of the Richmond wherein he lived. An "Enchanted Garden" has been created at the rear of the house, and outbuildings serve to exhibit paintings, photographs, manuscripts, and memorabilia of the poet's life. The Poe Museum is open to the public.

34

WILTON, HOME OF THE RANDOLPHS

Among the leading families of Henrico County and later of Richmond were the Randolphs. The family sprang from the union of William and Mary Isham Randolph, who about 1673 settled at Turkey Island in Henrico County on the James River, some ten miles below the present Richmond. "Between 1670 and 1691," wrote Philip Alexander Bruce in his *Social Life of Virginia in the Seventeenth Century*, "every official position in Henrico County was occupied by a member of the Randolph, Cocke, or Ferar families."

The Randolphs of Turkey Island generated a large and able family, whose members intermarried with most of the leading Tidewater planter families of the eighteenth century. In 1753 William Randolph III, grandson of the couple called "the Adam and Eve of Virginia society," built his own house on another James River promontory in Henrico. He called the house Wilton and adorned it with profits from his crops of tobacco, wheat, and corn.

In 1781 General Lafayette made his headquarters at Wilton for five days in May while attempting to withstand the invasion of Virginia by British forces under Cornwallis, coming north after their Southern campaign. Washington and Jefferson were guests of the Randolphs, among many others. The family had close ties with the Carys at Ampthill plantation across the James in Chesterfield County, the Byrds at Westover, the Harrisons at Berkeley, the Carters at Shirley, and other river families.

In 1933 the house was acquired by the Colonial Dames of America in the Commonwealth of Virginia and moved, piecemeal, to a site in Westhampton, west of commercial Richmond. There, provided with furnishings of the period, it serves as headquarters of the society which owns it. It is open to the public a part of each year.

36

THE CAPITOL OF VIRGINIA

Probably the most celebrated state capitol in the United States is the neo-classical temple which houses the office of the Governor and chambers of the General Assembly. Designed by Thomas Jefferson in the 1780s after a Roman temple at Nimes in France, it was the first public building in classical revival style in America. It gave rise to an epidemic of columned statehouses, courthouses, churches, and colleges which continue to be built across the United States.

The cornerstone was laid in 1785—two years after the final victory over Great Britain in the Revolution. For its day, the structure was not only revolutionary in style but also ambitious in size. Not until October 1788 was the building ready to receive the Virginia Assembly. Since that time, it has housed all regular sessions of that body. However, the Virginia Supreme Court of Appeals, once housed therein, has in this century moved to the nearby state Library and Courts Building on Capital Street.

President Jefferson Davis of the Confederacy and the congress of the Confederacy made use of the building from 1861 to 1865, when Richmond was the capital of the seceded states. The building's courtroom also saw the trial for treason in 1807 of Aaron Burr, with Chief Justice John Marshall presiding.

From 1904 to 1906 the building was enlarged with the addition of wings for the two bodies of the General Assembly. Since that time, however, public opinion has resisted further significant changes. Thousands of visitors yearly are shown through the building.

38

HOUDON STATUE OF GEORGE WASHINGTON

In designing the Capitol, Jefferson provided a rotunda to exhibit the splendid marble statue of George Washington which the Assembly had commissioned in 1784. At that time, Governor Benjamin Harrison V had asked Jefferson to engage a sculptor in Paris, and soon Jean Antoine Houdon had come to Mount Vernon to make a plaster bust of Washington and to take measurements for the rest of the figure.

The statue, which depicts Washington in Continental uniform, was completed in the sculptor's Paris studio. It arrived in Richmond in 1796, and it has since been recognized as the finest sculptured likeness of Washington in existence.

Around the statue, niches in the walls display busts of the seven other Virginia-born presidents, plus Lafayette. Funds for the latter were voted by the Assembly at the same time as for the Washington statue, "as a lasting monument of his merit and their gratitude." Like Washington's, it was the work of Houdon.

The busts of the other Virginia-born presidents were authorized by the General Assembly in 1930. They are Thomas Jefferson, James Madison, James Monroe, Zachary Taylor, William Henry Harrison, John Tyler, and Woodrow Wilson.

WASHINGTON STATUE IN CAPITOL SQUARE

On the grounds of the Capitol, a large equestrian statue of George Washington has become one of the city's most familiar sights. Its silhouette was chosen in the 1960s as the official insignia of the city of Richmond and is frequently reproduced.

The huge figure was sculpted during the 1850s in the prevailing French style of architecture by Thomas Crawford, who won the commission through a competition. The statue was unveiled in 1858.

Around the middle tier are figures of six other Revolutionary Virginians: Thomas Jefferson, Patrick Henry, George Mason, John Marshall, Thomas Nelson, and Andrew Lewis. Beneath them, allegorical figures at the base represent Independence, Revolution, the Bill of Rights, Justice, Finance, and Colonial Times. The monument is Virginia's tribute to the role of its people in the Revolution.

Elsewhere on the Capitol grounds are sculptured likenesses of other leading Virginians. These include Edgar Allan Poe, who grew up in Richmond and edited *The Southern Literary Messenger* there; Stonewall Jackson; Dr. Hunter Holmes McGuire, a Winchester surgeon who was Jackson's medical director; William "Extra Billy" Smith, governor of Virginia and a brigadier general of the Confederacy; and Harry Flood Byrd, a leading Virginia governor and senator of the 20th century.

THE GOVERNOR'S MANSION

Under the first constitution of Virginia as a commonwealth, in 1776, governors were elected for one-year terms, which could be renewed. Many early governors who served in Richmond, after the seat of government was moved there in 1780, filled the office only one year. In those austere days, the chief executive was responsible for renting his own house. In this casual style lived Governors Thomas Nelson Jr., Benjamin Harrison V, Patrick Henry, Edmund Randolph, Lighthorse Harry Lee, James Monroe, and others.

Governor John Tyler, father of the President of that name, recommended to the General Assembly during his term, from 1808 to 1811, that an executive mansion be built. It was completed in 1813, during the tenure of Governor James Barbour of Orange, and it has served ever since. After Appomattox it was occupied for five years by a military governor, but in 1870 its occupant was again an elected Virginia resident, as has been the case ever since.

Many leading Virginians have lived in "the Mansion," as it is called. They include John Tyler Jr., who later became president, Harry Flood Byrd, and in recent years Mills E. Godwin Jr. and John Dalton.

The Mansion's public rooms have recently been redecorated and refurnished in a style appropriate to its creation in 1813. Beautiful furniture and paintings have been given by individuals in an effort to show the style of life of the Old Dominion in the years of the early republic. The Mansion is opened to visitors at the convenience of the Governor.

44

WICKHAM HOUSE GARDEN

In the trial of Aaron Burr for treason in Richmond in 1807, one of the major participants was a polished Richmond attorney named John Wickham. He had come to Richmond from Long Island, married a local girl, and had become a leading attorney and a close friend of John Marshall. The Irish poet Thomas Moore described him as "fit to adorn any court."

Wickham created a public outcry when, on the eve of the trial, he invited both Marshall and Burr among a company of friends to dinner at his house. The incident provoked hot criticism from the Jeffersonian press.

Five years later, John Wickham built a house on Clay Street to a design by Robert Mills. Now preserved as part of the Valentine Museum of Richmond History, the Wickham House is a fine example of the Federal period in Richmond, though its furnishings also reflect the Victorian age which followed.

Wickham had been jailed as a Tory in the Revolution, when he enlisted in the British army in New York. At the close of the war, he studied in Europe and then in Williamsburg before coming to Richmond, soon after it had become Virginia's capital in 1780. In Richmond he married Elizabeth McClurg, daughter of Dr. James McClurg, a physician and a member of the Virginia delegation to the Constitutional Convention of 1787. They had 17 children.

Like most well-to-do Richmond households of its day, the Wickham house had a garden at its rear and outbuildings for servants and a carriage. Today the garden paths are lined with boxwood, and a fountain plays in its center. A large magnolia tree and other flowering trees and shrubs adorn the garden and shade the gallery at the rear of the house, where the Wickhams sat in mild weather. The house is furnished in period styles and is exhibited to the public.

46

THE VALENTINE MUSEUM

Few buildings in America preserve the Victorian tastes of the late 19th century better than the Wickham and Valentine houses, which form part of the Clay Street complex known as the Valentine Museum of Richmond History. Begun by Mann Valentine II in 1892 with a legacy of $50,000 and his handsome residence at Eleventh and Clay, it has subsequently been enlarged by the reconstruction nearby of the Cecil House, a 19th century townhouse moved from Fifth Street, and the acquisition of other structures.

The museum contains a unique library of Richmond manuscripts, photographs, prints, pictures, and books plus thousands of memorabilia of Richmond. Furniture, textiles, costumes, craft objects, household implements, hardware, and toys are among the artifacts collected. Few cities can boast so rich a hoard.

The heart of the museum is the Wickham House, built in 1812 by architect Robert Mills for attorney John Wickham, a leading Federalist attorney and friend of John Marshall. Its guests have included John Marshall, General Winfield Scott, and William Thackeray. The spacious house, with box-lined garden and rear galleries, is one of the finest mansions of the Federal period in the nation. Its circular staircase is especially admired, as are the floor-length windows which look onto the garden and the bow room at the rear of the house.

As the home of Mann Valentine II in the Victorian era, the house was furnished in the best style, and this is reflected in its furnishing today. In leaving the structure to the city as a museum, Valentine also left his collection of local history, Indian material, and archeological and anthropological specimens. To this have been added sculptures and studio furnishings of his brother, Edward Virginius Valentine, whose work includes the recumbent statue of Lee at Lexington.

The Valentine Museum is open daily to visitors.

HOME OF JOHN MARSHALL

Ever since it became the capital of Virginia in 1780, Richmond has attracted some of the nation's leading lawyers. The eminent George Wythe came from Williamsburg soon after 1780 to become a judge, while Edmund Randolph at about that time became a local attorney.

No Richmond lawyer, however, has ever achieved more distinction than John Marshall, who settled here after the Revolution. He married Mary "Polly" Ambler, and about 1790 built a house at Ninth and Marshall Streets, in the new "Court End" of town. A brick structure of Federal style, it incorporated the latest decorative features of the era. An adjoining office was used by Marshall to interview his clients, read his casebooks, and write notes for trial use.

Marshall's appointment by John Adams in 1801 to be chief justice did not change the simple, democratic lifestyle of John and Polly Marshall. Because of his wife's ill health, Marshall often did the marketing and household chores. He was a popular figure among Richmond's men in the Quoit Club at Buchanan's Springs, near the 1000 block of West Broad Street.

In his long lifetime, tall and gangling John Marshall was a familiar figure in Richmond. When he died in 1835 in Philadelphia, his body was brought to Richmond for burial beside his wife in Shockoe Cemetery.

In 1911 the house was loaned by the city to the Association for the Preservation of Virginia Antiquities, which has protected it against the bulldozers which have levelled most of 18th century Richmond. Through the generosity of friends, the house has been refurnished in the style which its builders gave it in their lifetime. In the 1970s a renovation returned the house to its original form. The house is open to the public.

INTERIOR OF THE MARSHALL HOUSE

Two styles of decoration popular in early Virginia blend in the house of Polly and John Marshall, still standing at Ninth and Marshall Streets. They are the Georgian style of the 18th century, so popular in the early Tidewater plantations, and the Federal style which had a later vogue.

The front parlor is typical of the panelled walls and marble faced mantels which graced the homes of such Richmond worthies as the Mayos, Adams, Seldens, McClurgs, Carringtons, Fishers, Foushees, and Randolphs. A profile portrait of Marshall by Saint Memin hangs over the mantel, while a Turkey carpet covers the floor.

The Marshalls were active in the life of Richmond from the 1780s until he died in 1835. As Chief Justice, he presided over the trial of Aaron Burr for treason at the Capitol in 1807. He occasionally attended plays at the Richmond Theatre until it burned in 1811, and he was chairman of the committee which built Monumental Church as a memorial to its victims. He headed a city committee to develop the James River-Kanawha Canal, designed to increase trade from the Ohio Valley to Richmond.

Though a cousin of Thomas Jefferson, whose presidency from 1801 to 1809 ran concurrently with the early years of Marshall's chief magistracy, the two men were politically and personally opposed. Had President John Adams not elevated Marshall by his "midnight appointment" just before Adams left office in 1801, Jefferson would have appointed Spencer Roane, a brilliant Jeffersonian adherent in Richmond, who was chief justice of the Virginia Supreme Court. In Roane's lifetime, his court frequently questioned decisions of Marshall's.

52

LINDEN ROW HOUSES

The dominant architectural style of early Richmond was classical revival. This was popularized in America when the Capitol at Richmond was built in this style at Jefferson's behest, leading to countless columned and pedimented buildings throughout the thirteen original states.

The style was embraced in the construction of many residences and row houses in Richmond, and it is evident in surviving early structures along such early streets as Main, Grace, Cary, Franklin, Marshall, Clay, and Leigh. A fine example—the best of the row houses surviving among the 20th century commerce of the downtown—is Linden Row on a block of East Franklin Street facing the Public Library.

Linden Row was built about 1847 by Fleming James. It consists of a series of handsome Greek Revival houses built of brick and adorned with columned doorways. Two of the original buildings were removed in 1922 to make way for the Medical Arts Building.

Built at a time when row houses were popular in America, Linden Row is reminiscent of projects in Baltimore, Washington, Boston, and other eastern cities. Relatively narrow, the Linden Row units each contains an English basement and three above-ground storeys. Once popular as residences and as private schools, the buildings are now principally antique shops and offices.

Before the Civil War the Southern Female Institute was conducted in two of the houses by D. Lee Powell. After the war, Mrs. Sophronia "Phronie" Pegram and her daughter Mary, later Mrs. Joseph R. Anderson, conducted the well-known girls' school which became Miss Jennie Ellett's school and is today St. Catherine's.

54

OLD HALL OF HOUSE OF DELEGATES

Until the Capitol was enlarged in 1906, the House of Delegates met from 1788 onward in a pilastered chamber with the Speaker's table at center and the members' desks on either side. Several important Virginia constitutional conventions were held in this chamber. So also were sessions of the Confederate Congress in 1861-65 and of the "Underwood" Constitutional Convention of the Reconstruction Era, which gave new opportunities to blacks and to public education in 1869-70.

However, the most memorable event to take place in the chamber was Robert E. Lee's acceptance of command of Virginia's forces there on April 23, 1861. Having declined field command of Federal forces in the Civil War and resigned his U.S. Army commission, Lee was offered the Virginia post by the Virginia convention which in April 1861 voted secession.

In accepting, Lee spoke these brief words:

"Mr. President and Gentlemen of the Convention: Profoundly impressed with the solemnity of the occasion, for which I must say I was not prepared, I accept the position assigned me by your partiality. I would have much preferred had your choice fallen on an abler man. Trusting in Almighty God, an approving conscience, and the aid of my fellow citizens, I devote myself to the service of my native State, in whose behalf alone will I ever again draw my sword."

The room today contains a larger than life standing figure of Lee in Confederate uniform, plus busts of other leading Virginians and a standing figure of Henry Clay, who was born near Richmond. It is open to the public.

SAINT PAUL'S CHURCH

Intimately tied to the history of Richmond and of the Confederacy is St. Paul's Episcopal Church, one of the oldest and most beautiful churches in the city. It was there on Sunday, April 2, 1865, that President Jefferson Davis of the Confederacy received a dispatch from General Robert E. Lee telling of the fall of Petersburg and the necessity to move the Confederacy's headquarters from Richmond.

Davis left the church, and soon the supplies and records of the Davis government began to move by wagon train across the James River and southward. Much of the city's warehouse area along lower Main Street and the James River was burned to keep supplies from Federal troops.

Built in 1845 after the style of St. Luke's Church in Philadelphia, St. Paul's was a handsome Greek Revival structure with a towering steeple; the steeple was later replaced. The new church was formed by members of Monumental Episcopal Church.

For many years the pews of St. Paul's were owned by families, as had been done in Anglican churches in the United States and in Great Britain. They paid annual "pew rent" to provide for upkeep of the church. On the day following the dedication by Bishop William Meade, the pews of the Church were "sold" at auction to various families of the congregation. Ninety-three pews were disposed of at prices ranging from $100 to $860, for a total of $43,000. Within a month the rector could tell his congregation their church had been paid for.

Funeral services for John Tyler were held at St. Paul's after the ex-President died while attending the Virginia Secession Convention in 1861.

Another historic downtown church which survives with an active congregation is Second Presbyterian Church. However, most early congregations have built new churches in the west end of the city.

58

THE JAMES RIVER AND KANAWHA CANAL LOCKS

Two locks of the old James River Canal have recently been preserved as a footnote to Richmond's history. They are Locks 4 and 5 of the Tidewater Connection, which once enabled tobacco boats to circumvent the falls of the James by using the canal southward from Bosher's Dam to the lower end of Richmond, seven miles away.

Unearthed by Reynolds Metals Company in the 1960s in excavations for a building at Twelfth and Byrd Streets, they have been rebuilt and put on exhibit along with the old 13th Street Bridge over the canal, built in 1860 by the merchants Richard Haxall and Lewis Crenshaw, proprietors of the Haxall-Crenshaw Flour Mill.

These are reminders of George Washington's ambitious plan, in 1784, for a "Great Central American Waterway," to stretch from the Atlantic to the Rocky Mountains. Washington got the support of Governor Benjamin Harrison V, and the General Assembly in 1785 incorporated a State-subsidized company for "clearing and improving the navigation of the James River."

By 1789 the company had completed a canal around the falls of Westham, then just west of Richmond, and another from the river into the city. It was the first canal system in North America, though soon to be eclipsed by the Erie Canal on the Great Lakes, which in 1824 opened the floodgates for midwestern shipments to New York City.

Despite recurrent damage by floods and mud slides, the canal system was extended by 1840 westward to Lexington. By 1851 it reached Buchanan County, and a canal was projected to link it with the Kanawha River in western Virginia. Then came the Civil War, and the canal slowly died, to be superseded by railways.

Other Richmond features of the canal system are visible along the James in lower Richmond, and enthusiasts hope someday to incorporate them in a scenic park. The locks at Twelfth and Byrd are open to the public from 9 to 4:30 each Tuesday through Saturday.

WHITE HOUSE OF THE CONFEDERACY

The pace of Richmond life quickened on April 17, 1861, when Virginia seceded. The city realized it would be a strategic center in the war, and fortifications were begun. On May 29, Jefferson Davis, president of the Confederacy, arrived from Montgomery and established Richmond as capital of the seceded states. The Davis family stayed at the Spotswood Hotel at the southeast corner of Eighth and Main Streets.

Richmond's city council offered the Davises the use of a handsome mansion at Clay and Twelfth Streets, overlooking Shockoe Valley. Davis declined the offer, however, and the Confederacy rented the house for him, rather than accept it free. Formerly the residence of Dr. John Brockenborough, president of the first Bank of Virginia, the structure is preserved as the White House of the Confederacy. It is a part of the Museum of the Confederacy, which is open daily.

The Davis family lived and occasionally entertained in the house from 1861 through 1865, when the Confederate government left Richmond in April to avoid capture. However, President Davis was apprehended at Irwinville, Georgia, a month later and imprisoned at Fort Monroe, awaiting trial for treason. He was later released and lived in New Orleans until his death at 81 in 1889. His body was later returned to Richmond's Hollywood Cemetery.

Designed as a two-storey mansion by Robert Mills, the White House of the Confederacy was later given a third storey. Although it presents a stern front facade on Clay Street, its rear facade is embellished with a columned portico. Recently a separate museum has been built to exhibit objects of Confederate interest, preserved by the Confederate Memorial Literary Society, organized in Richmond in 1894.

INTERIOR OF JEFFERSON DAVIS'S WHITE HOUSE

What chiefly distinguishes Richmond from other Southern cities is its indelible traces of the Confederacy, which made its headquarters here in the Civil War. When Richmonders speak of "the war," they still refer to the times of Robert E. Lee, Stonewall Jackson, and Jefferson Davis. Indeed, many still refuse to call it "The Civil War" and prefer "The War of Northern Aggression" or "The War of Southern Secession."

Memories of those years are numerous in the Capitol Hill area, which was the city's vortex in the years when Federal forces tried to breach Richmond's defenses and destroyed the Southern secession. Among the chief reminders are Robert E. Lee's house at 707 East Franklin Street, battlefields in Henrico, Chesterfield, and Charles City counties, and many monuments.

Nowhere else is so much Confederate lore brought together as in the Museum of the Confederacy, which occupies Jefferson Davis's erstwhile White House at Twelfth and Clay streets. In it and in a modern museum addition, the Confederate Memorial Literary Society has assembled thousands of flags, letters, uniforms, pictures, and other memorabilia of the war and of its grey-clad participants.

Among its items are the sword and uniform worn by Lee when he surrendered the Army of Northern Virginia at Appomattox Courthouse, the Colt revolver of Jefferson Davis, and numerous memorabilia, swords, and firearms. The museum is open daily.

64

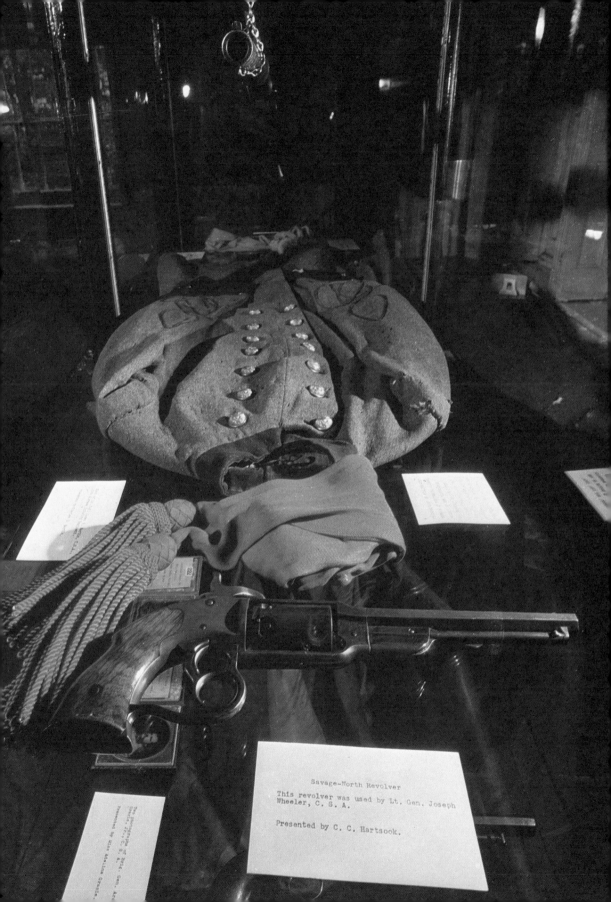

Savage-North Revolver

This revolver was used by Lt. Gen. Joseph
Wheeler, C. S. A.

Presented by C. C. Hartsook.

THE FAN DISTRICT AND VIRGINIA COMMONWEALTH UNIVERSITY

Once a decaying "inner city", downtown Richmond has recently been revived. Its turn-of-the-century Fan District has been enlivened especially by the phenomenal growth of Virginia Commonwealth University—now an institution of 20,000 students.

VCU began life as a shoestring operation of the College of William and Mary. Its 1917 Richmond School of Social Work and Public Health utilized converted houses along Franklin Street and Park Avenue. Training in the fine arts and the liberal arts was soon added. In 1968 the State linked the resultant Virginia Commonwealth University and Medical College of Virginia in one vast urban university, its two campuses separated physically but joined by overall administration. Called Virginia Commonwealth University, the institution's Medical College of Virginia is now its Life Sciences Division.

This view of the Fan District and environs shows part of Richmond's new east-west Downtown Expressway in foreground with Cary and Main Streets paralleling its course. Between the latter may be seen several of the large new buildings of the VCU academic campus, including James Branch Cabell Library, the Life Sciences Building, the School of Business, and Oliver Hall for science and education courses.

Wrote Thomas F. Hall and William Westbrook in their book, *The Fan*: "And if the residents enjoy the university, the students enjoy the unique environment of the Fan. There are cobbled alleys and yard sales and parks for rock concerts. There are grand weddings and simple celebrations to commemorate past history. And there are tours to bring the students inside the life here even more."

Several new commercial buildings are underway in the blighted area between Main Street and the James River, part of which is shown in the foreground here. Once again the James is playing a part in Richmond as the focus of city life.

66

HOLLYWOOD CEMETERY

High above the banks of the James, near the section of downtown Richmond known as Oregon Hill, is Hollywood, the city's largest and best-known cemetery. Dedicated in 1849, it is the resting place of presidents John Tyler and James Monroe, whose tomb is shown here, as well as of Jefferson Davis, president of the Confederacy. Because of its rolling hills, beautiful trees and shrubs, and many quaint and handsome memorials, it is among the most famous and most beautiful burial places in the United States.

Residents of the city who died in its early years were usually buried in the yard of St. John's Church, completed in 1741 to serve as the church of Henrico Parish. There are buried such early figures as George Wythe and Elizabeth Arnold Poe, mother of Edgar Allan Poe.

Later cemeteries were Shockoe, where John Marshall and members of his family are buried, and Oakwood, on the eastern end of Richmond, where some 18,000 victims of the Seven Days' Battles of the Civil War in the spring of 1862 were buried in a period of several weeks.

One of the earliest burials in Hollywood was of James Monroe. After his death in New York in 1831, he was laid to rest there. However, sentiment for his burial in Virginia led in 1858 to removal of his remains to a handsome tomb in Hollywood. Because of mounting sectional feeling, newspapers took occasion to point to Virginia's gift to the nation of Monroe and others in the genesis of the republic.

Monroe's grave was visited in 1860 by the 19-year-old Prince of Wales, Albert Edward, who was to succeed his mother, Queen Victoria, as Great Britain's monarch upon her death in 1901. Travelling under the name "Baron Renfrew," the prince came to Richmond on October 7, 1860.

68

ROBERT E. LEE ON TRAVELLER

Richmond is notable for the charm of its neighborhoods. The most ambitious of these in the 19th century was Monument·Avenue, which has since ceased to be suburban by its absorption into the central city.

What makes Monument Avenue notable is its central vista of tree-bordered grass and the succession of statues which decorate the thoroughfare: statues of Lee, Jeb Stuart, Jefferson Davis, Stonewall Jackson, and Commodore Maury. The ambitious concept took years to carry out, beginning in the 1880s and ending in 1929 with the placement of the Maury statue west of the Boulevard. They helped give Richmond an unusual grandeur of scale.

The Lee statue, unveiled at a Confederate gathering on May 31, 1890, set the pattern for Monument Avenue. Much squabbling between factions inside and outside Richmond preceded it, however. The choice of a sculptor was a hot issue, and General Jubal A. Early threatened of one early design, "If the statue of General Lee be erected after that model [I will] get together all the surviving members of the Second Corps and blow it up with dynamite."

City fathers long pondered the best site. Hollywood Cemetery? Libby Hill? Capitol Square? Monroe Park? Finally, a site in a then open field was chosen, destined to become the intersection of Monument and Allen avenues. The statue was executed by the French sculptor Antonin Mercie; its $77,000 cost was raised by Southerners.

A last-minute crisis developed when Governor Fitzhugh Lee insisted that Lee should tower as high as Crawford's statue of Washington did in Capitol Square. The ten additional feet added $6,000 to the cost.

The statue was faced south so that Lee would forever face the region he had fought for.

70

JEB STUART'S STATUE ON MONUMENT AVENUE

The deification of Confederate leaders continued well into the twentieth century in Richmond, as Monument Avenue attests. There in 1907 were unveiled the statues of both General Jeb Stuart and of Jefferson Davis in ceremonies a few days apart.

Stuart ranks next to Lee and Jackson in Richmond's heart because the cavalry leader had been shot in battle six miles north of Richmond in 1864 while defending Richmond. Brought to the home of his brother-in-law, Dr. Charles Brewer, at 206 West Grace Street, he died soon afterward. Only 31 and a daring soldier, he had won the devotion of the Southern people. His death, only a year after Stonewall Jackson's, left Richmond heartbroken.

His funeral at St. James's Episcopal Church brought out a great crowd of mourners. "At the head of the coffin sat the soldier who had rescued him, all battle-stained and soiled," wrote Richmond's Judith McGuire, "and nearby the members of his staff, who all adored him."

Stuart's statue, by Fred Moynihan, shows the cavalryman with plumed hat and prancing steed. The ceremonies were part of a week-long reunion of 18,000 Confederate veterans, whose worn and faded battle flags brought tears to the eyes of those last survivors.

John Buchan, Lord Tweedsmuir, governor-general of Canada and British novelist, wrote in 1924 that Richmond's "memorials of the War Between the States are conceived with such dignity and simplicity that they are infinitely the most impressive things I saw on the American continent."

LOOKING ACROSS THE JAMES

The first business of Richmond was the James River. Even today—three centuries after the first William Byrd came from England to live on the south shore—the river's edge seems part of an earlier and slower age.

Looking northward across the James at Ninth Street (Mayo's) bridge, one sees in the foreground warehouses of earlier years, lining the mid-channel Mayo's Island. Beyond is one of the sections of the James which was deepened in earlier centuries for use of tobacco boats. In the background, rising from low hills which surround the James, are the offices and factories of modern Richmond.

Skyrocketing land values downtown in the 1960s and 1970s have led to increasing highrise buildings. They have also restored to more productive use many formerly blighted blocks along Main, Cary, and Byrd Streets in downtown Richmond. The current "Main to the James" development program has upgraded a wide area. The creation of the Downtown Expressway, paralleling the James, has ventilated the old city by changing traffic patterns and opening up new vistas. And the development of a neglected area at James River Plaza by creation of the new and majestic Federal Reserve Bank promises to further revolutionize the downtown.

74

HOTEL JEFFERSON

The center of social life in the 1890s was lower Franklin Street, where many town houses competed in elegance with the Commonwealth Club and the Hotel Jefferson. Of them all, the hotel was the largest and most spectacular. Built by Major Lewis Ginter at a reputed cost of $1,500,000, and designed by the celebrated architects Catrere and Hastings, it simulated the Romanesque buildings of Europe then so popular with American architects. Its two towers were modelled on those of the Giralda in Seville.

Though engulfed by current auto traffic, the Jefferson continues to attract admiration. Its lobby is one of the handsomest to be seen in America, and its soaring grand staircase was used for a scene in the film, "Gone With the Wind." Its interior masonry, sculptures, paintings, and ceilings attract visitors who enjoy Edwardian elegance. Many civic and social organizations make their headquarters in the proud building.

No Richmonder did more for his city than did Lewis Ginter, a tobacco and real estate millionaire who died in 1897. Born in New York of a Dutch immigrant family named Guenther, he came to Richmond in the 1840s as a linen merchant. After serving in the Civil War, he became a principal in the tobacco firm of John F. Allen and directed it toward making the newly-popular cigarette. The firm of Allen and Ginter after 1875 produced "Richmond Gems," which obtained a worldwide market. After Allen's retirement, Ginter merged his company with James B. Duke's American Tobacco Company.

A bachelor, Ginter built a mansion at Shafer and Franklin Streets which is now part of the campus of Virginia Commonwealth University. He planned the area that became Ginter Park and gave 25 acres of it as the site of the Union Theological Seminary. But the Hotel Jefferson is peculiarly his monument.

76

GARDENS OF AGECROFT HALL

The English tone of Richmond life has been noted by Dickens, Thackeray, and other British visitors from colonial times. Admiration for Virginia's mother country has led even to the importation of English houses. Two of them were brought across the Atlantic in the 1920s and reassembled in the west end suburb of Windsor Farms.

The first was Agecroft Hall, which was dismantled in 1926 in Lancaster-shire, England, and erected by T.C. Williams, Jr. in 1928 as his residence. On a nearby site, Alexander Wilbourne Weddell in the same era used materials from the former Warwick Priory, once built near Stratford, in a house, half of which is a partial reproduction of Sulgrave Manor, the onetime house of the Washington family, in England. Both houses are among Richmond's adornments today.

The gardens of Agecroft Manor lie behind the house, with the James River and its south shore spread majestically beyond. Both house and gardens are open to visitors.

Agecroft Manor is a Tudor mansion built originally in 1490. After serving for a half century in Richmond as a private Richmond residence, it has in recent years been exhibited as a museum.

78

VIRGINIA HOUSE IN WINDSOR FARMS

The heights along the James River in the west end are lined with handsome houses. There are situated Agecroft Manor and Virginia House, two medieval English houses which were brought over from England in the 1920s and '30s and reconstructed on Virginia soil.

Virginia House, now owned by the Virginia Historical Society, was disassembled in the 1920s and moved to Windsor Farms by the late Mr. and Mrs. Alexander Wilbourne Weddell, A onetime American ambassador to Spain and the Argentine, Mr. Weddell found the house at Warwick, near Stratford-on-Avon in England, in the 1920s.

Built as the Priory of St. Sepulchre in the 12th century, the stone building was given by King Henry VIII when he seized England's monasteries in the 16th century to Thomas Hawkins, one of his favorites. In 1572 Queen Elizabeth I visited the priory with the Earl and Countess of Warwick.

As rebuilt in Richmond, the house utilizes major portions of the priory but orients part of them so as to reproduce the lines of Sulgrave Manor, the English house of the Washingtons, near Stratford-on-Avon. Mr. Weddell named the structure Virginia House in honor of his wife and his state. On their death in 1948, the Weddells left the house, its furnishings, and several millions to the Virginia Historical Society, which exhibits the house to the public and utilizes it for meetings and receptions.

VIRGINIA MUSEUM OF FINE ARTS

At the depth of the 1930s Depression, Virginia courageously took the first steps to create the first state art museum to be built in the nation. Today—50 years later—the Virginia Museum of Fine Arts is a nationally-known institution which has stimulated a wave of painting, sculpture, acting, and musical performance in Virginia.

Located strategically on the Boulevard between Kensington and Grove Avenues, the Museum is a showplace of the world's art. A 600-seat theatre, a performing studio, two restaurants, and a lively art rental and purchase service are among its many features.

An offer of his collection of paintings plus $100,000, made by John Barton Payne to the Commonwealth of Virginia through Governor John Garland Pollard in the early 1930s, was the germ from which the museum grew. Payne specified that the gift be matched by another $100,000, and Governor Pollard adroitly got it from private donors and the Federal government.

Begun in a handsome structure of French Renaissance style, the museum has grown more contemporary through additions. Meanwhile it has steadily added to its old master paintings and sculptures, its post-impressionist collection, and its modern art and art deco. In its theatre are offered a choice of plays, chamber music concerts, dance recitals, and lectures.

The museum was brought to nationwide repute during the 20-year tenure of talented director Leslie Cheek Jr., whose fastidious attention to every phase of the museum's design, production, and publication gave it distinction. Under his direction, the museum launched tours of Virginia by its Artmobiles and publication of *Art in Virginia* and other periodicals.

Today the Museum is increasing its research and holdings in American art and decoration, particularly in the realm of Virginia and the South.

UNIVERSITY OF RICHMOND

The campus of the University of Richmond lies close to the James River in Richmond's west end. There, surrounding an extensive lake, are the brick Tudor buildings of Richmond College and its coordinate women's school, Westhampton College.

Familiar to all Richmond alumni is the Frederic W. Boatwright Memorial Library, shown here, honoring a scholar who brought the small school from a Baptist men's college in 1895 to a modern coeducational university on his retirement from the presidency in 1946. The library and its tower were built in 1955. An addition was completed in 1976.

Founded in 1832 as a seminary for Baptist ministers, the institution moved to Richmond in 1834. Named Richmond College in 1840 and broadened in purpose, it grew rapidly under Dr. Robert Ryland. In 1870 it added a law school. In 1914 it absorbed the former Richmond Female Institute to create Westhampton College for women.

In recent years the university has been strengthened by an unprecedented gift of $50,000,000 from E. Claiborne Robins, Richmond pharmaceutical manufacturer. The institution has widened its scope, terminating Baptist control over its policies and adding a school of business administration, a graduate school, and a program of adult education.

The 350-acre campus in Westhampton has been developed with a lake as the focal center. The university today enrolls more than 5,000 students.

84

WORLD WAR I CARILLON

The largest and most frequented of Richmond's parks is Byrd Park, close to the James River at the Boulevard. Its lake and landscaped acres provide a haven for waterfowl as well as for tennis and baseball players.

Thrusting skyward from the park's center is Virginia's World War I Memorial Carillon, a monument built with funds provided by the Virginia General Assembly and by a Citizens Committee, which raised $75,000 to buy the carillon bells. The city of Richmond provided the site and landscaped it with plaza, walkways, and decorative trees and shrubs.

The carillon is played on special occasions, and visitors are permitted to view the interior and the mechanism. Begun in 1926, the project was completed in the 1930s.

CIVIC AND MEDICAL CENTERS

Broad Street has remained Richmond's chief commercial thoroughfare from Jeffersonian times to the present. Near its eastern end range the principal civic and medical buildings of the city, including the 18-storey City Hall, built in 1972, and the hospital and principal buildings of the Medical College of Virginia, now a part of Virginia Commonwealth University.

This aerial view, looking westward from a segment of the Richmond-Petersburg Turnpike in the foreground, reveals the continuing role which Shockoe Bottom, the "Court End" of the old town, plays. Among the foreground buildings are several of the five hospitals associated with the Medical College. Nestled among them is the Egyptian Building, the oldest structure of the MCV campus, which is used as an auditorium and a microbiology center.

At Ninth and Marshall streets, across from City Hall, can be seen the John Marshall house, surviving from the 1790s. Behind it, close to the Federal Building and municipal parking facilities, is Richmond Coliseum.

The four east-west arteries shown are, from left to right, Broad Street, Marshall Street, Clay Street, and Leigh Street. Once a residential section of early Richmond, this area declined in the twentieth century. Much of it has been cleared in recent urban rehabilitation projects to allow for the Richmond-Petersburg Turnpike, for Interstate 64, and for growing State and local services.

88

RICHMOND COLISEUM

Richmond took a new turn in 1971 when it opened a spectacular Coliseum in the center of a former market and produce area. The domed structure is part of a Civic Center which includes municipal offices and extensive parking. In the offing, according to city plans, are hotels, restaurants, and stores to enliven the old downtown area, once disdained as the "wrong side" of Broad Street because of the saloons permitted to operate there.

The development is directed toward bringing to Richmond large conventions, touring theatricals, major sports events, and other business-generating attractions. The ultimate object is to halt the obsolescence of the downtown and draw residents from suburbia back into the heart of the city.

The Coliseum contains 12,000 seats in 35,000 square feet of air-conditioned space. Its floor can convert from an ice hockey rink to a basketball court. It can also become a circus arena, an auditorium, banquet hall, or dance floor.

Major sports events take place frequently in the Coliseum. An East Coast Invitational Indoor Track Meet is held there each January, a World Championship Tennis Tournament each February, and other events at other times.

SKYLINE OF RICHMOND

Richmond today presents an imposing array of towers against the sky.
Beginning in 1930 with the Central National Bank on Broad Street, its sky-
scrapers increased greatly in the 1970s.

Among the structures visible on the skyline here are the City Hall, the
Medical College of Virginia, the Federal Reserve Bank, First and Merchants
Bank Building, and the Life Insurance Company of Virginia Building.

92

COMMERCE SURROUNDS THE CAPITOL

The special quality of Richmond is respect for the past. Nowhere is that more evident than in Capitol Square, in the old downtown section of the city. There the State Capitol stands, timelessly, in an oasis of trees and grass—a relic of Jeffersonian days. All around it rise the skyscapers of banks, insurance companies, and State offices. It is an oasis in a busy modern city.

Like nearly all east coast communities, Richmond's growth has been upriver, away from the port village which was laid out in the 1730s at the falls of the James. But the downtown in the 1970s still remains vital, thanks to the growth of State, Federal, and local governmental offices there.

Capitol Square is a State enclave. Around the Capitol are now a dozen modern high-rise offices. Unfortunately, the Capitol's vista south to the James has been blocked by Main Street buildings.

The congestion of traffic grows acute each January and February, when the General Assembly meets. In recent years this has brought hordes of onlookers: demonstrators, lobbyists, proponents, and opponents. Many policemen are now required to control crowds. School children come in a steady stream aboard yellow school buses. Virginia's government, long kept lean by the thrift of the Byrd Organization, has now become large.

The aroma of tobacco often fills the air of the Capitol in warm weather. It comes from warehouses and cigarette plants on "Tobacco Row," an area along lower Main Street. This and the Victorian fronts of Main Street offices seem incongruous among high-rise buildings. But it is typical of Richmond, where today and yesterday rub elbows.

94